ENCOUNTERING EMMANUEL

A GUIDED ADVENT JOURNAL FOR PRAYER AND MEDITATION

HEATHER KHYM

ILLUSTRATED BY JOSIAH HENLEY

AVE MARIA PRESS AVE Notre Dame, Indiana

Visit **www.avemariapress.com/private/page/ encountering-emmanuel-resources** for more information about bulk discounts, a leader's guide, help with organizing a small group, videos from Heather Khym discussing the theme for each week of Advent, and other resources to help you make the most of your time together with *Encountering Emmanuel.*

Nihil Obstat: Reverend Monsignor Michael Heintz, PhD
Censor Librorum
Imprimatur: Most Reverend Kevin C. Rhoades
Bishop of Fort Wayne–South Bend
Given at Fort Wayne, Indiana, on 9 April, 2024

The *Nihil Obstat* and *Imprimatur* are official declarations that a book or pamphlet is free of doctrinal or moral error. No implication is contained therein that those who have granted the *Nihil Obstat* or *Imprimatur* agree with its contents, opinions, or statements expressed.

Founded in 1865, Ave Maria Press is a ministry of the United States Province of Holy Cross.

www.avemariapress.com

Paperback: ISBN-13 978-1-64680-367-5

E-book: ISBN-13 978-1-64680-368-2

Cover image © 2024 Josiah Henley, heartofiesvs.etsy.com.

Cover and text design by Brianna Dombo.

Printed and bound in the United States of America.

CONTENTS

INTRODUCTION

BEHOLD, NOW IS THE ACCEPTABLE TIME; BEHOLD, NOW IS THE DAY OF SALVATION.

2 CORINTHIANS 6:2

In all its splendor and wisdom, the Church provides distinct liturgical seasons through which the entire mystery of Christ unfolds for us. Each season invites us not only to meditate on particular mysteries but to allow God's truth, beauty, and goodness to become incarnate in our lives. Today we find ourselves at the beginning of Advent and have an opportunity to approach this Advent like no other Advent. Instead of this Advent being part of the routine of this time of year, what if it was an occasion for something new, something deep, something that could change everything? I'd like to propose that this is indeed what this Advent will be, if we approach with an open heart to encounter Emmanuel like never before.

Let us begin by focusing our attention on the pivotal moment in history when, two thousand years ago, Jesus Christ took on flesh and became one of us. At the same time, let's look forward with joyful hope to his Second Coming, when he will come again to judge the living and the dead. Over the next four weeks, as we hold these two very important realities, we will be invited to encounter the living Christ, who wants his coming to be personal and real in each of us right here, right now.

In other words, Advent is not just a time to prepare for Christmas, and Christmas is not meant to be experienced only on December 25. Every single day is a preparation for the coming of Christ, and every day is an occasion to respond to God in our midst, receiving his presence being birthed into whatever circumstances we find ourselves in. The kingdom of God truly is at hand.

A common temptation in our spiritual lives is to allow our heads to connect to an idea and let it stay as an idea, but not allow it to seep into our hearts and become an authentically lived experience, an experience that leads to conversion and deeper intimacy with God. This Advent journal is an attempt to help you move from familiar concepts of Jesus's coming to an experience of him coming into your particular circumstances—your longing, fears, hopelessness—and changing everything with his presence.

Recall Luke 1:28–38 where we read about the Annunciation. We read that an angel appeared to Mary and announced that she would conceive, and the Savior would be born to her, to which Mary gives her full *yes*. As we ponder this epic moment in human history, we are not meant to meditate on Mary only to understand her experience, but also to allow her experience to show us how to live. Scripture helps to explain our lives and God's unique desires and plans for each person. Just as God desired to make a home for himself within the womb of Mary, the Savior wants to come to you, to be born into every area of your life. God will not force—he asks—and we have a choice. Just as Mary welcomed the Savior, will you open wide your heart this Advent and give your fiat as she did?

Pause and imagine that right where you are in this moment, God sends an angel with a similar announcement to you. The angel stands before you and says, "Do not be afraid! *You* have found favor with God. He has looked upon *you*, even in your lowliness, and has news of great joy. The Savior is to be born within *you*. Emmanuel desires to come into every part of you—into your heart, your mind, your life, your brokenness, your pain—and bring his light, his love, his peace, his hope, and his healing. He wants to make an exchange with you: your sorrow for joy, your anxiety for peace, your darkness for light, your bondage for freedom."

My hope and prayer this Advent is that just as Mary said yes to the invitation for Christ to be incarnate in her womb, we, too, will say yes to the Savior to be born in us, to experience and encounter Emmanuel, God with us. He is the one we need, the one we seek, and the one who is coming to us today. And so we begin.

HOW TO USE
THIS JOURNAL

The *Encountering Emmanuel* Advent journal combines daily meditations, questions for reflection, journaling space, prayers, and beautiful original art to draw you into a deeper, richer experience of Advent. It helps prepare you not only to experience the joy of Jesus's birth, but to open your life to the Incarnation of Christ in a personal way.

Over the next four weeks, we will explore the four reasons for the Incarnation as taught in the *Catechism of the Catholic Church* (*CCC* 457–60). First, Jesus came to save us from our sin and reconcile us to the Father. Second, he came to make us sharers in his divine life through our adoption as sons and daughters of God. Third, he came to show us how to live through his model of holiness. Fourth, Jesus came to reveal the depth of God's love for us.

As we embark on this journey together, we have a unique opportunity set before us to encounter Emmanuel and to have profound experiences of Jesus being born into the most personal places of our hearts, minds, and lives. Through the meditations, prayers, scriptures, and real-life stories found in this journal, you will be invited to slow down, to reflect, to prepare, and to create space for daily encounters with Jesus.

WHO IS *ENCOUNTERING*
EMMANUEL FOR?

Encountering Emmanuel is for anyone who desires to experience the Advent season as a healing journey that leads you to explore the crevices of your heart. The season of Advent is the ideal time to step back from your life and evaluate where you stand with God, yourself, and others. This Advent journal provides a daily path to prayer and reflection for healing and restoration. *Encountering Emmanuel* was designed for use in a group setting. There is something special about taking this Advent journey with a community, whether that community is your entire parish, a small group, or your family. Visit **www.avemariapress. com/private/page/encountering-emmanuel-resources** for more information about bulk discounts, a leader's guide, help with organizing a small group, videos from Heather Khym discussing the theme for each week of Advent, and other resources to help you make the most of your time together with *Encountering Emmanuel*.

You can also use *Encountering Emmanuel's* meditations and journaling prompts on your own, to help you draw near to God, hear his voice in new ways, and pour out your heart to him as you turn your attention daily to the mystery of Christ who dwells within you and desires to enter into every place that has not yet encountered the birth of his presence. You may find that this Advent, you're in special need of regular quiet times of connection with God; *Encountering Emmanuel* is an excellent way to help you find that space each day.

HOW IS *ENCOUNTERING* *EMMANUEL* ORGANIZED?

Encountering Emmanuel is organized into four parts:

✢ In week 1, you'll focus on the first reason that Jesus came, which is to save us. In our sin, humanity was utterly lost and incapable of saving ourselves. The Father sent his Son to rescue and save us, doing for us what we could not do for ourselves in order to restore our relationship with him. Each meditation will reveal places that we need to experience the saving power of Christ.

✦ In week 2, you'll reflect on the second reason that Jesus came, which is to make us sharers in his divine life. God desires oneness with us and has destined us to participate in his divine life. Each day you will meditate on specific and tangible ways that God gives us opportunities to participate in his divine life through how we live out our identity as adopted sons and daughters and our relationship with him. We will close each day by expressing our desire to have our lives be one with Jesus.

✦ In week 3, you'll focus on the third reason that Jesus came, which is to show us how to live. When we examine the way Jesus lived, we see that he has given keys for us to experience life in its fullness. Each day we will meditate on one of these keys and invite Jesus to reveal to us the path to becoming fully alive.

✦ In week 4, you'll deeply explore the fourth reason that Jesus came, which is to show us God's love. Christ is the full revelation of the love the Father has for us. The Father is not passive or distant, and he sent Christ, love incarnate, to enter into every part of our human experience and show the depth of his love.

Within each week, you'll encounter a simple daily pattern made up of the following parts:

✦ Each day opens with a *quotation* from a saint, a great teacher, or scripture in order to focus your thoughts on the key idea from that day's meditation.

✤ The *meditation* from Heather Khym draws out a message from scripture, the *Catechism of the Catholic Church*, and real-life examples that helps us understand Christ's desire for deeper union and places within us that have not yet encountered his presence.

✤ An important aspect of our Advent preparation for the Savior's coming is to journey within and see the places that are empty and in need of him; a single-line or *breath prayer* is included at the end of each meditation to help you invite him in. At the end of the journal, you'll find all of these prayers compiled into a Litany of Encounter. Feel free to begin praying the entire litany as soon as you feel ready, and carry it with you beyond the Advent and Christmas seasons.

✤ The *reflection* challenges you to ponder and journal in response to the meditation, helping you identify practical ways to live out the Advent season more fully.

✤ Finally, after you've read and journaled, the closing *prayer* provides a starting point for your own requests and prayers of thanksgiving and praise to God.

HOW SHOULD I READ ENCOUNTERING EMMANUEL?

This Advent journal's daily format is flexible enough to accommodate any reader's preferences: If you're a morning person, you may want to start your day with *Encountering Emmanuel*, completing the entire day's reading, reflection, journaling, and prayer first thing in the morning. Or you may prefer to end your day by using *Encountering Emmanuel* to focus your attention on Christ as you begin to rest from the day's activities. You may even decide to read and pray as a family in the morning and journal individually in the evening.

The key is finding what works for you, ensuring that you have time to read carefully, ponder deeply, write honestly, and connect intimately with the Lord in prayer. Whatever approach you choose (and whether you decide to experience *Encountering Emmanuel* with a group or on your own), be sure to visit www.avemariapress.com/private/page/ encountering-emmanuel-resources for extra resources to help you get the most out of this special Advent journey.

FIRST WEEK
OF ADVENT

JESUS,
SAVE US

FIRST WEEK OF ADVENT

SUNDAY

AWAKE, MY SOUL, AWAKE!
SHOW THY SPIRIT, AROUSE
THY SENSES, SHAKE OFF THE
SLUGGISHNESS OF THAT DEADLY
HEAVINESS THAT IS UPON THEE,
BEGIN TO TAKE CARE FOR THY
SALVATION. LET THE IDLENESS
OF VAIN IMAGINATIONS BE PUT
TO FLIGHT, LET GO OF SLOTH,
HOLD FAST TO DILIGENCE.

ST. ANSELM OF CANTERBURY

HE COMES TO WAKE US FROM OUR SLEEP

Liturgical seasons in the Church are an incredible gift for us. Not only do they give us a structured framework to help us intentionally focus our personal and communal worship, but they can become an experience of reawakening to the truth, beauty, and goodness of God that is all around us.

We live in a world saturated with materialism, instant gratification, and constant noise, making it all too easy for us to slip into a state of spiritual lethargy, becoming numb to God's presence in our lives. We might find ourselves feeling directionless or worthless. Or maybe we just feel constantly distracted and have developed a restless spirit—a sense that something isn't quite right in our lives. No matter how spiritual lethargy looks, the season of Advent can serve as a divine alarm clock to rouse us to the real mystery of salvation that is unfolding in the world and within each of our personal stories of redemption.

There is a sobering quality to Advent, amid the warmth of lights and carols being sung, that the Church is proclaiming loud and clear, "Wake, oh sleeper—the Savior has come! Repent and believe—the Savior is here! Prepare the way—the Savior is coming again!" Just as the shepherds and the wise men responded to the sign of the star, we, too, are called to follow the light of Advent that leads us to encounter the person of Jesus.

This Advent, let's not allow it to come and go without a profound reordering of our affections and attention so that we can become transformed by the love of Christ. For this to occur, we will need to be willing to do our part to be honest and open, willing to surrender all that stands in the way of deepening our relationship with Jesus. As we light the candles on the Advent wreath, let each flicker be a reminder that Christ is the true Light that dispels the darkness, and he is waking us from our slumber to the profound reality of his presence, love, authority, and relentless pursuit of our hearts.

Where I need to be awakened, *Jesus, be born in me.*

REFLECT

1. What are things you engage in that cause lethargy in your spiritual life?
2. What truths do you desire to awaken to?
3. What do you desire from this Advent season?

_____

_____

_____

_____

_____

_____

_____

_____

_____

_____

PRAY

DEAR JESUS, I WANT TO WAKE UP TO THE BEAUTY AND REALITY OF WHO YOU ARE. PLEASE SHOW ME THE PLACES IN MY LIFE THAT ARE KEEPING ME FROM YOU, SO THAT I CAN WELCOME YOU MORE DEEPLY INTO MY HEART THIS ADVENT. JESUS, SAVE ME. AMEN.

MONDAY

I HAVE COME INTO THE WORLD
AS LIGHT SO THAT WHOEVER
BELIEVES IN ME MAY NOT REMAIN
IN DARKNESS.

JOHN 12:46

HE COMES INTO THE DARKNESS

If you were anything like me as a child, you were terrified of the dark. I had the typical concern that a scary monster might jump out to get me. I was so comforted when a light was turned on and the darkness dissipated along with my fear.

The lighting up of darkness was and still is one of my favorite things about Christmas time in the Northern Hemisphere. Although the nights are longest in December, the comforting glow of Christmas lights dispels the dark. Nostalgia washes over me as I recall the multicolored incandescent lights on our house, shining like little embers of hope in the night. During Christmastime as a kid, my fear of the dark was replaced with anticipation for evening to arrive, so I could experience the brilliance of the lights. Only when there is darkness can we experience the real comfort, wonder, and beauty of the light.

In John's gospel, Jesus announces that he is the Light of the World. He comes crashing through the darkness of night into a world darkened with sin. A star illuminates the way—a star that he breathed into existence and that echoed the truth of who he is, the Light in whom there is no darkness (see 1 John 1:5).

Many of us have outgrown our need for nightlights, but we are still afraid of the dark—or what hides in it. Darkness doesn't just exist in the physical world when the lights are extinguished; it also exists within our hearts and minds. All of us have dark places, where the light of Christ has not yet come.

Maybe it's sin, an addiction, a wound, self-loathing, unforgiveness, shame, judgment, fear, or a belief that we are unlovable. These dark places can reside in a heart that has other areas that have been touched by God and already experienced the exodus from slavery to freedom, where we have answered the call of he who has called us "out of darkness into his marvelous light" (1 Pt 2:9). But Jesus isn't content with only part of us living in the light. He wants our whole being to be in the light. The light is where he is; it's *who* he is. When we live as children of light, we experience the freedom we were made for. Don't be afraid of the dark, for Christ our Light has come and is coming, in all your dark places.

Where I am in darkness, *Jesus, be born in me.*

REFLECT

1. When have you experienced the comfort of light in the darkness?
2. What is one area in which the light of Christ has touched your life?
3. What is one area of darkness in your heart where you desire the light of Christ?

_____

_____

_____

_____

_____

_____

_____

_____

_____

PRAY

_DEAR JESUS, YOU ARE THE LIGHT
OF THE WORLD, AND THERE IS
NO DARKNESS IN YOU. I WANT TO
RESPOND TO YOUR INVITATION TO
COME OUT OF DARKNESS AND LIVE
AS A CHILD OF THE LIGHT. PLEASE
GIVE ME STRENGTH AND COME WITH
YOUR HEALING, LOVE, AND FREEDOM.
JESUS, SAVE ME. AMEN._

FIRST WEEK OF ADVENT

TUESDAY

IN EVERYTHING GOD WORKS
FOR GOOD WITH THOSE WHO
LOVE HIM, WHO ARE CALLED
ACCORDING TO HIS PURPOSE.

ROMANS 8:28

HE COMES AS THE PROMISE

When my husband and I were studying theology at Franciscan University, we had opposite approaches to our work. While I waited until the last moments to "feel inspired" and stay up all night to finish, Jake was already done and relaxing because he had planned ahead. He had methodically worked through his outline and was completely at ease. He was clear on where he was headed, with each step carefully laid out to arrive at its completion. I'm so grateful that God doesn't operate like me, with a random and haphazard approach. From the beginning of time, God had a clear plan. He made a covenant with us, he knew exactly what his goal was, and he knew that Jesus Christ would be the consummation of his promise. Nothing was left to chance.

In the tapestry of human history, the threads of covenant and prophesies are woven together and culminate in Jesus as the fulfillment of God's divine plan. The Old Testament is filled with ache and anticipation as it prophesies the coming of a messiah, the chosen one destined to bring redemption and restoration. From the beginning of Genesis, where we hear that the serpent's head would be crushed, to the words of Isaiah, foretelling a virgin conceiving Emmanuel, the stage was set for the arrival of the Promised One. Only God could weave such an intricate tapestry across generations that brought his plan to fulfillment in Jesus Christ. Nothing was careless.

In the little town of Bethlehem, the culmination of centuries-long anticipation took on flesh. Jesus comes as the embodiment of God's faithfulness to his plan. The manger held not just an infant, but the answer to the deepest longings of humanity—God's promise wrapped in swaddling clothes. Ancient prophesies echoed through the life and teachings of Jesus. The blind received sight, the lame walked, and the captives were set free—a resounding affirmation that God's promises were not just words but living realities in the person of Jesus. Nothing was random.

In the quiet of our hearts, may we reflect on the profound truth that Jesus is the culmination of God's promises—the reason for our hope in God's faithfulness. As we navigate the current difficulties of life, let us find comfort in knowing that we have a loving God who keeps his promises and he will carefully bring to completion his unique plan for us.

Where I doubt your promises, *Jesus, be born in me.*

REFLECT

1. When you consider the intricacies of salvation history, what stirs in you about the character of God?
2. What barriers do you have to trusting that God has a plan for your life?
3. How can you take a step toward greater trust with one area of your life?

PRAY

*ALMIGHTY GOD, FROM THE BEGINNING
OF TIME YOU HAVE HAD A PLAN FOR ME
AND MY LIFE. HELP ME TO TRUST THAT
YOUR PLANS ARE GOOD AND THAT YOU
WILL LEAD ME TO THE FULLNESS OF
JOY. JESUS, SAVE ME. AMEN.*

WEDNESDAY

GRACE IS NOT OPPOSED TO
EFFORT, IT IS OPPOSED TO
EARNING.

DALLAS WILLARD,
THE GREAT OMISSION

HE COMES WITH POWER

In the Gospel of Matthew, we hear about a rich young man who comes to Jesus and asks, "What good deed must I do, to inherit eternal life" (Mt 19:16)? It's here, in his question, that I would like us to pause and reflect. The man wants to know what *he* can do to inherit eternal life, and when Jesus invites the man to move beyond what he can accomplish on his own, to what is possible only with Christ, the man walks away sad. Here we find the gap in his spiritual life and relationship with God, one that resonates with our own struggles.

The rich man has earned material wealth, and his earning, or self-sufficiency, extends into his spiritual life and practice too. He is used to operating on his own power to succeed and either doesn't know how to live from a posture of dependence on God or doesn't know how to ask for help. He prefers to ask God for answers that can assist him in independently earning his way forward, instead of humbly asking for God's power that can help him exchange his weakness for divine strength, making the impossible, possible. Answers aren't bad, but until answers move us to deeper conversion, repentance, and reliance on God, we will continue to walk away from following Jesus in our independence.

In a technological age, where everyone is looking for answers and assistance in navigating life more easily, we can be tempted to engage with God similarly. We come to him asking him merely to be our assistant, instead of inviting him to be Lord of our lives and to use us as instruments for his divine purposes. God didn't come to be our personal assistant; he came to save us and bring us into communion with him, so that we might have access to his divine life and power and live from the truth that we are children of a good and capable Father. It begins with surrendering our self-reliance, admitting our need for him, and opening ourselves to his life and power. As Pope Benedict XVI says, "This power, the grace of the Spirit, is not something we can merit or achieve, but only receive as pure gift. God's love can only unleash its power when it is allowed to change us from within" (Twenty-Third World Youth Day Homily, Randwick Racecourse Sunday, July 20, 2008).

Where I am self-reliant, *Jesus, be born in me.*

REFLECT

1. In what areas of your life do you operate with a spirit of self-reliance?
2. Where do you need God's divine power in your life?
3. What is something you do not have the power to do that you'd like to surrender to God?

_____

_____

_____

_____

_____

_____

_____

_____

_____

_____

PRAY

LORD OF ALL POWER, I NEED YOU.
I ADMIT THAT I AM NOT STRONG
ENOUGH AND NEED TO LEARN HOW
TO BE DEPENDENT ON YOUR POWER
BEING ACTIVE IN MY LIFE. PLEASE
CHANGE MY HEART FROM ONE OF
INDEPENDENCE TO DEPENDENCE ON
YOU. JESUS, SAVE ME. AMEN.

FIRST WEEK OF ADVENT

THURSDAY

FOR FREEDOM CHRIST HAS SET
US FREE.

GALATIANS 5:1

HE COMES TO SET US FREE

I recently participated in an escape-room experience. The concept is a team gets locked in a room, and to get out they find clues and work through a series of riddles to free themselves. At our latest attempt, we experienced one major problem: we couldn't crack the first clue. We finally gave up and admitted to the staff we were stuck. They told us where to find the first key, but when we went there, there was no key. The staff arrived shortly, key in hand, and apologized because they forgot to put the key back into the game before we started. Without that key, there was no way to get ourselves out without someone intervening.

In scripture, God intervenes in miraculous ways to do for people what they cannot do for themselves; he sets them free from real captivity. He parts the Red Sea, rescues Daniel from the lion's den, heals the leper, and releases Paul and Silas from prison with an earthquake. God does the impossible.

In our lives, we find ourselves in all kinds of prisons that we are incapable of escaping alone: chains of addiction, a captive heart hardened to love, unforgiveness that binds, or our minds shackled with lies about ourselves, God, and others. Our prisons within are any place where we are not truly free. Often, we have tried to free ourselves with no success, so we settle for coping or we just give up.

A first step to remedy our despair is to ask for the gifts of faith and hope. These two virtues are free gifts given by God, not something achieved or earned. Faith is the belief in who God is, the Savior who has the power to set us free. Hope is our trust in the promises of God, promises that we are no longer slaves, but rather God's children who have access to his power through Jesus. Jesus doesn't just have the key to unlock our prisons—he is the key. Freedom begins when we invite God into our locked places, and he comes with everything he is. Scripture tells us that it is "for freedom [that] Christ has set us free" (Gal 5:1).

Jesus is the only one who has won true freedom for us and who has the power to break every chain, bondage, and place where we are locked within. He has come, and he is here to set *you* free.

Where I am held captive, *Jesus, be born in me.*

REFLECT

1. What is one place in your life right now where you are not free?
2. What do you desire Jesus to do about that?
3. What is holding you back from stepping into freedom?

_____

_____

_____

_____

_____

_____

_____

_____

_____

_____

_____

_____

PRAY

*JESUS, YOU CAME TO SET CAPTIVES
FREE, AND I AM A CAPTIVE. PLEASE
COME INTO THE PLACES OF BONDAGE
IN MY LIFE AND BRING TRUE FREEDOM.
JESUS, SAVE ME. AMEN.*

PRONE TO WANDER, LORD, I
FEEL IT, PRONE TO LEAVE THE
GOD I LOVE; HERE'S MY HEART;
O TAKE AND SEAL IT; SEAL IT FOR
THY COURTS ABOVE.

**ROBERT ROBINSON, "COME THOU
FOUNT OF EVERY BLESSING" (1758)**

HE COMES TO RECONCILE US

One scripture that I cherish depicts the Good Shepherd, who leaves the ninety-nine sheep to go after the one that is lost. Imagine the scene. It's late afternoon and the sun is beginning to descend behind the rolling green hills. Rocks are scattered across its surface like a mosaic, and a herd of sheep is grazing there. The shepherd stands amid them, his eyes surveying the surroundings. He pauses as he notices that a sheep is missing. His eyes dart across the horizon where he sees the sheep entangled in a thicket. The shepherd knows the herd is safe and recognizes that he needs to move urgently to get to the sheep, so he runs. He finds the sheep trapped and distressed, so with careful hands, he untangles it from the thicket, mindful of every movement to prevent further panic and entanglement. And suddenly, it's free. Knowing how exhausted and stressed the sheep is, the shepherd lifts it onto his strong shoulders and carries it back to safety.

We often think this scripture is about ninety-nine people who are close to Jesus and one who is far away. This is true, but let's imagine that all one hundred sheep represent parts of you. Have you ever thought, "A part of me feels this, but another part of me feels differently"? These opposing feelings reveal that we aren't fully integrated; we are incongruous. When we place this concept as a lens over our relationship with God, we discover that there are parts of us that have encountered him and experienced conversion, and parts of us that are still far away and unreconciled. Parts of us still have not yet met the love of the Father, Jesus the Savior, or the Holy Spirit the Comforter. Faith and doubt, confidence and fear, virtue and vice reside in tension within the same heart. We prefer to focus on the parts of us that choose moral living and often minimize or hide the parts that are terrified, faithless, despairing, and wandering.

Jesus didn't come for part of us. He wants all of us. With the same care the shepherd has for the lost sheep, Jesus wants to carefully restore every part of us to full communion with him, ourselves, and one another. We all have parts that have wandered and need to be rescued and reconciled to the Father through Jesus our Good Shepherd.

Where I am unreconciled, *Jesus, be born in me.*

REFLECT

1. What causes you to wander away from Jesus?
2. Try to imagine that you are the sheep that is lost and stuck in the thicket. What does the thicket represent?
3. Spend a few minutes journaling about the parts of you that feel terrified, faithless, or despairing. When you're done, ask Jesus the Good Shepherd to come and sit with each of those parts of you, and allow yourself to experience his loving presence.

_____

_____

_____

_____

_____

_____

_____

_____

_____

_____

PRAY

JESUS, YOU HAVE COME TO RECONCILE US TO THE FATHER. I CONFESS THAT THERE ARE PARTS OF ME THAT HAVE WANDERED FROM YOU AND ARE ENSNARED. JESUS, PLEASE RESCUE THE LOST PARTS OF ME AND CARRY ME HOME TO YOU. JESUS, SAVE ME. AMEN.

FIRST WEEK OF ADVENT

SATURDAY

IN THE WORLD YOU HAVE
TRIBULATION; BUT BE OF GOOD
CHEER, I HAVE OVERCOME THE
WORLD.

JOHN 16:33

HE COMES INTO
A WORLD AT WAR

One of my favorite films of all time is *Braveheart*, partly because my whole family hails from Scotland so my ancestral pride wells up, but even more so because of how the story pinpoints the realest parts of life, love, and suffering. It doesn't sugarcoat the terrors of war, yet it also elevates the hero—one who was willing to lay down his own life for the truth and the ones he loves.

We, too, find ourselves in a world at war, physically and spiritually. Nations are rising against each other, institutional corruption abounds, children are starving, families and communities are broken, and people are trafficked. Scripture also tells us of the spiritual battle, that "we are not contending against flesh and blood, but . . . against the spiritual hosts of wickedness" (Eph 6:12). These things can overwhelm us and leave us feeling helpless.

In *Mere Christianity*, C. S. Lewis said, "Christianity agrees . . . this universe is at war." At the time of his birth, Jesus comes into the middle of a war. Herod is murdering newborn boys because he fears the Messiah will take his throne, and turmoil abounds. From the moment of the Fall, there has been a physical and spiritual battle.

The hope of the Incarnation, and for us this Advent, is that Jesus comes into the middle of the war in the most unsuspecting disguise. No one suspected the Warrior King would sneak in as a fragile baby, or that he comes not just to fight but to win. What was true two thousand years ago remains so today: Jesus comes to us amid a multitude of battles. He wants to come into the physical wars and simultaneously into the wars raging in our own minds—the ones that leave us feeling divided, overwhelmed, and insecure.

Most wars happen because two sides believe opposing things. We have places in us that believe two different things, where lies and false beliefs are taking over truth and the enemy is beating us down, hard. There is a battle over the throne of your heart, and the Prince of Peace comes to speak his peace and truth into the chaos. Jesus is not a weak and impotent God, but a warrior with the power to bring peace to the chaos within. He has already laid down his life and defeated the power of the enemy; will you allow him to do that in you?

Where I am losing the battle, *Jesus, be born in me.*

REFLECT

1. What is one battle that is going on in your heart and mind right now?
2. Take a moment to write down what the lie is in that battle. Ask Jesus what the truth is that he wants you to know.
3. What would you experience if that battle was over and peace entered in?

_____

_____

_____

_____

_____

_____

_____

_____

_____

_____

_____

PRAY

*JESUS, PRINCE OF PEACE, COME INTO
THE BATTLE IN MY MIND AND HEART.
I ASK THAT YOU BRING YOUR TRUTH
TO DISPEL THE LIES AND REINTEGRATE
THE SEPARATED PARTS OF MYSELF.
JESUS, SAVE ME. AMEN.*

SECOND WEEK OF ADVENT

JESUS, MAKE US SHARE IN DIVINE LIFE

SECOND WEEK OF ADVENT

SUNDAY

LET US LOVE, SINCE THAT IS
WHAT OUR HEARTS WERE MADE
FOR.

ST. THÉRÈSE OF LISIEUX

HE COMES INTO A FAMILY

I have dear friends who got married with a desire to welcome children. After many painful years of infertility, they decided to open the door to adoption. The first call came one morning: "We have a baby boy. Do you want to bring him home?" They said yes and welcomed their son. Hearts were knitted together, and their family grew. The second call came two years later: "A baby girl is being born. Do you want to bring her home?" Again, they said yes, and an ocean of love enveloped the four. They now had the "perfect family," a boy and a girl, but God was not done yet. Several years later, God invited them to open their hearts again. They got a call: "Will you bring two more home?" They said yes, and four became six. Unbreakable bonds formed, and an abundance of love filled their home. A year later we went for dinner, and they told us their family was growing again. "You're adopting!" I exclaimed. Smiles crept across their faces, and after more than twenty years of infertility, I heard these words for the first time: "No, we are pregnant!" Tears of joy poured onto the restaurant table, but the God of Miracles wasn't done yet. Six years later they opened their home to another boy. The two are now eight lives woven together in love, each unique soul on its journey toward eternity within a family.

Jesus could have come into our world in any fashion, but he chose to come as a child into a family. He came into an earthly family because God is a family. The Trinity is a communion of persons, each pouring out and receiving the gift of the other. This is the image that we were made in: a family of life and love.

Through the revelation of the Trinity and the Holy Family, Jesus is teaching us about a foundational reality necessary for our thriving. We are made for relationships, and we are made for family. Family can look like a lot of different things; whether it's biological, through adoption, or spiritual bonds of love, we are invited to belong and have others belong to us. You and I are not made to be alone. Through our baptism, God has adopted us into his family. He chose you, he opened his heart and his family to you, and you belong. No matter what the circumstances of your earthly family are, your real origin is the Trinity, a family of love.

Where I need familial love, *Jesus, be born in me.*

REFLECT

1. What do you think of when you think of family?
2. What do you want to ask Jesus to restore in your understanding and experience of family?
3. How do you feel when you hear the truth that you belong to Jesus and to his family?

_____

_____

_____

_____

_____

_____

_____

_____

_____

_____

PRAY

*JESUS, I BELONG TO YOU, AND YOU
BELONG TO ME. THANK YOU FOR
INVITING ME INTO YOUR FAMILY
AND FOR MAKING MY HEART FOR
RELATIONSHIPS WITH OTHERS. HELP
ME TO LOVE OTHERS AND RECEIVE
LOVE MORE DEEPLY. JESUS, I WANT TO
SHARE IN YOUR DIVINE LIFE. AMEN.*

SECOND WEEK OF ADVENT

MONDAY

LET JESUS PRESENT IN THE
BLESSED SACRAMENT SPEAK TO
YOUR HEARTS. IT IS HE WHO IS
THE TRUE ANSWER OF LIFE THAT
YOU SEEK. HE STAYS HERE WITH
US: HE IS GOD WITH US.

**POPE JOHN PAUL II,
ADDRESS TO YOUNG PEOPLE
OF BOLOGNA, SEPT. 27, 1997**

HE COMES TO BE OUR FOOD

The richness of scripture is one of the reasons I always return to the Bible when I'm feeling lost. There are tens of thousands of connections between the Old and New Testaments, and God is speaking in all the details. He has the most beautiful way of taking something simple and making it profound.

With your imagination, zoom in on the stable in Bethlehem, and try to visualize the things you have heard from Nativity narratives. We see a stable, the Holy Family, animals, shepherds, swaddling clothes, and a manger. Let's zoom in further on the manger.

A manger is a feeding trough for animals, yet this trough quickly becomes the crib where Jesus is laid. What a profound reality and mystery that Jesus, who calls himself "the Bread of Life," is laid in a place where creatures are nourished with food. But he doesn't stop there. The word *manger* in French means "to eat," and if that wasn't enough, *Bethlehem* in Hebrew means "house of bread." Doesn't God write the most beautifully true and exceptional stories? Through his reiteration, we can conclude that he's trying to communicate something for us to live and understand.

Why would Jesus be born into a city called House of Bread, be laid in a feeding trough, and later call himself the Bread of Life if he didn't desire with all of his heart that he would be our food and that we would literally consume him as our daily bread in prayer, in his Word, and in the Eucharist?

Jesus comes to nourish us and to meet us in our deepest hunger, but if we're honest, we often go elsewhere to be fed, and we are left starving. No amount of success, affirmation, winning, hustling, and accumulating will ever touch this deep place of hunger. It's a place in us that only God can satiate. In all of our wanderings, we are always desperate for Jesus. This aching cry is expressed so beautifully by St. Augustine, who after tasting all the things the world could offer finally encounters God and says, "You called, you shouted, and you broke through my deafness. You flashed, you shone, and you dispelled my blindness. You breathed your fragrance on me; I drew in breath and now I pant for you. *I have tasted you, now I hunger and thirst for more.* You touched me, and I burned for your peace" (*The Confessions*, emphasis added).

Where I hunger for more of you, *Jesus, be born in me.*

REFLECT

1. Do you believe that Jesus can fully satisfy you?
2. What are you afraid that he won't satisfy, and why?
3. How can you make time in your weekly schedule to receive Jesus in the Eucharist more often?

PRAY

*JESUS, YOU COME AS FOOD TO
SATISFY EVERY LONGING THAT I HAVE.
HELP ME TO REJECT THE ILLUSION OF
WORLDLY SATISFACTION AND COME TO
YOU WITH ALL OF MY DESIRES. JESUS,
I WANT TO SHARE IN YOUR DIVINE
LIFE. AMEN.*

SECOND WEEK OF ADVENT

TUESDAY

I SHALL DO EVERYTHING FOR
HEAVEN, MY TRUE HOME.

ST. BERNADETTE

HE COMES TO
MAKE A WAY TO HEAVEN

When my kids were little, they liked to ask a lot of questions—so many that I often had to tell them that we were taking a fifteen-minute question break just so I could breathe. One of the most prominent questions over the years has been "Why?" It would come again after every answer, bringing us down a rabbit hole as my kids attempted to push their understanding of why something was the way it was.

If we don't know the "why" behind our Christian life, this life can turn into a lot of things that aren't necessarily about Jesus or following him. It can easily become a routine, a social group, or a place of obligation. It's important to ask the questions. Why do we go to Church? Why deny our worldly desires? Why do we pursue holiness? Why do we try so hard to turn away from sin? Answers like "It's the right thing to do" or "I don't know" aren't going to suffice. If we don't know the real answer and have it in our sights as the goal, then our hearts will quickly lose motivation and at the very least become bitter about how hard living as a Christian is. There is only one worthwhile answer, and it is heaven.

Heaven is the place of total union with God, where all of our pain, shame, sorrow, suffering, and guilt are wiped away and we experience the fullness of joy in his presence. Pope John Paul II says that heaven "is neither an abstraction nor a physical place in the clouds, but a living, personal relationship with the Holy Trinity. It is our meeting with the Father which takes place in the risen Christ through the communion of the Holy Spirit" (General Audience, July 21, 1999).

We may picture heaven as an eternal church service in the sky, but honestly, that sounds boring after a hundred years with eternity to go. We can't fathom the satisfaction and joy that we will experience in heaven as we rest in deep intimacy with the Trinity: no more striving, no more proving, no more grasping. Our joy will be complete. Jesus has come to make a way for us to be with him forever in heaven. Let this be the goal that we set our eyes upon.

Where I need the hope of heaven, *Jesus, be born in me.*

REFLECT

1. What do you think of when you imagine heaven?
2. What are you looking forward to the most?
3. What can you do to keep heaven at the forefront of your motivations in life?

_____

_____

_____

_____

_____

_____

_____

_____

_____

_____

_____

PRAY

*JESUS, IT'S EASY FOR ME TO FORGET
THAT HEAVEN IS MY DESTINATION
AND TRUE HOME. PLEASE PURIFY MY
MOTIVES, AND HELP ME TO KEEP YOU
AT THE CENTER OF MY HEART. JESUS, I
WANT TO SHARE IN YOUR DIVINE LIFE.
AMEN.*

AND PREACH AS YOU GO, SAYING, "THE KINGDOM OF HEAVEN IS AT HAND." HEAL THE SICK, RAISE THE DEAD, CLEANSE LEPERS, CAST OUT DEMONS.

MATTHEW 10:7-8

HE COMES WITH A MISSION

In the book of Isaiah, there is a beautiful prophecy about the mission of the Messiah. This prophecy was repeatedly proclaimed in synagogues by the Jewish people throughout history. I can only imagine when hundreds of years after it was written, a man named Jesus stood up in the synagogue, picked up the scroll with this scripture on it, and read aloud, "The Spirit of the Lord is upon me, because he has anointed me to bring good news to the poor. He has sent me to proclaim release to the captives and recovering of sight to the blind, to set at liberty those who are oppressed" (Lk 4:18). But unlike every other time this had been read, it was followed up with one pivotal declaration. Jesus said, "Today this Scripture has been fulfilled in your hearing" (Lk 4:21). Can you imagine the shock and confusion on their faces? Was he telling them that he was the Messiah who had come to accomplish this? That is exactly what he was telling them, and I imagine they couldn't take their wide eyes off of him.

Jesus comes to give our lives meaning and purpose as he invites us to participate in his mission. A purpose-filled life is never lived for the satisfaction of oneself, but rather for the love and service of God and others, for something greater than ourselves.

Christ's mission for us is not dependent on what our state in life is, our occupation, our age, our gender, or our status. No matter where we find ourselves, we are each called to heal the blind, set captives free, and raise the dead through the power of Christ active in our lives through our Baptism. No one is disqualified from this call.

It's a common lie from the enemy for people to believe they are not worthy, that they are unfit, too sinful, not enough, too much, or anything that could make them doubt their ability to participate in this mission. The truth is that we are lowly, yet we have been invited, forgiven, infused with divine power, and made worthy by Christ's blood to be Jesus in the world. God wants people to be set free, to be healed, to see clearly, to be raised to life from their sin and sorrow, and he has chosen you and me to accomplish this.

Where I need to live your mission, *Jesus, be born in me.*

REFLECT

1. How are you currently living out Christ's mission in your life?
2. Are there any lies that you believe about why you are not worthy or able to participate in Christ's mission?

PRAY

DEAR JESUS, I AM IN AWE THAT YOU WOULD INVITE ME TO SHARE IN YOUR MISSION. PLEASE COME AND FILL ME WITH YOUR PRESENCE AND WITH YOUR HOLY SPIRIT, SO THAT I CAN LIVE OUT THIS CALL WITH FAITHFULNESS, PERSEVERANCE, AND LOVE. JESUS, I WANT TO SHARE IN YOUR DIVINE LIFE. AMEN.

SECOND WEEK OF ADVENT

THURSDAY

HE IS TRULY THE SON OF GOD
WHO, WITHOUT CEASING TO BE
GOD AND LORD, BECAME A MAN
AND OUR BROTHER.

*CATECHISM OF THE CATHOLIC
CHURCH, 469*

HE COMES AS OUR BROTHER

When our kids were little we would take them out for breakfast after Mass. One Sunday at the restaurant, a woman we knew stopped to say hello. Our four-year-old looked at the woman with her big blue eyes. "Do you know who I am?" she asked. The woman replied, "I don't know your name," then with a smile toward us she continued, "but I know who you belong to."

I'd like to express a similar sentiment to you. I may not know who you are, but I know who you belong to. As we reflected earlier this week, family is tied together with relational bonds either through blood, adoption, or spiritual adoption. Because of our Baptisms, you and I are family.

Most of us have been told that God is our Father and have devoutly prayed the "Our Father," but we don't often reflect on how the reality of this relationship has taken place. *Abba* isn't just a nice sentiment; God is truly our Father. We are his real adopted sons and daughters, which means that Jesus, the Son of God, is our brother. Let that sink in for a moment: the Messiah is your brother, and therefore we have the same Father.

Have you ever considered that when God the Father looks at Jesus and then looks at you, he sees you as the same? We are equally his children. His love is the same; the parent/child bond is the same. Jesus affirms this in his prayer to the Father: "I in them and you in me, that they may become completely one, so that the world may know that you have sent me *and have loved them even as you have loved me*" (Jn 17:23, emphasis added). What immense humility that God the Son would come down to become one with us, thus elevating us to be partakers in his divine life. Christ has drawn us into his family, where his Father becomes our Father.

We have been raised higher than the angels and given an unimaginable gift to share in his life, "for the Son of God became man so that we might become God" (St. Athanasius). May we never doubt our dignity and worth with the knowledge that Christ our brother reveals our Father. We have a mother, Our Lady, and we are family with the Communion of Saints. The divine is alive in you.

Where I need you as my brother, *Jesus, be born in me.*

REFLECT

1. What stirs in your heart when you reflect on Jesus as your brother?
2. How could the knowledge that we are participating in divine life change how you view yourself and others?
3. What is one thing you desire from Jesus as your brother?

_____

_____

_____

_____

_____

_____

_____

_____

_____

_____

PRAY

_JESUS, I WANT TO YOU KNOW YOU,
NOT ONLY AS LORD, BUT AS MY
BROTHER. THANK YOU FOR BRINGING
ME INTO YOUR FAMILY. HELP ME TO
SEE GOD THE FATHER AS MY TRUE
FATHER. JESUS, I WANT TO SHARE IN
YOUR DIVINE LIFE. AMEN._

SECOND WEEK OF ADVENT

FRIDAY

I WILL OPEN MY HEART TO YOU;
PUT THY DIVINE FIRE INTO IT.
YOU ARE A FLAME, AND LET
MY HEART BE TURNED INTO A
FLAME!

ST. GEMMA GALGANI

HE COMES TO SET
THE WORLD ON FIRE

Last summer we went away for a few days with friends at their lakeside cabin. It was a beautiful setting with tall evergreens creeping right up to the water and on the other side layers of tall mountains that sat against the backdrop of a beautiful blue sky. One afternoon, we caught the scent of smoke, and we knew that a forest fire had started nearby. By the time night had fallen, half of the mountain across the lake was ablaze. We stood on the back porch and watched in shock as the wildfire spread. Tree after tree erupted into flames, launching fiery pine cones like grenades into the trees below, igniting more fires with every explosion. The power and intensity of the fire was unbelievable.

Fire is depicted in many different ways throughout scripture. We read about the burning bush, the pillar of fire that led the Israelites, the fire Abraham built to sacrifice Isaac, the refiner's fire, and the poignant words of the author of the Letter to the Hebrews describing God as "a consuming fire" (Heb 12:29). Fire signifies God's presence and is the means to purify, illuminate, and transform.

In Luke 12:49, Jesus declares, "I came to bring fire upon the earth; and would that it were already kindled!" Jesus wants the world to be set ablaze with the Holy Spirit and the fire of his pure love. This begins with an individual heart. Jesus comes to set your heart on fire with his love, so that you can spread it to every cold and weary heart you encounter.

What if we let the fire of God illuminate, burn away, transform, and consume us with love so we become his fire that lights up the world? What if this fire could melt away all our duplicity and set us free to become truly who we are made to be, the image of love himself? And what's the alternative? To not be consumed by God's fire of love? To become bored and half-hearted, regretting our mediocrity because we know deep in our hearts we are made for more?

You and I are made for more. If we desire fullness of life with Jesus, it requires stepping into the flames. The moment we do and the fire begins to burn in us, we are able to bring others into the same fire. Is this not what heaven will be, souls consumed with God's fire of love forever?

Where I need your consuming fire, *Jesus, be born in me.*

REFLECT

1. What part of your heart do you need Jesus to purify with his fire?
2. What part of your life do you need Jesus to illuminate with his fire?
3. What holds you back from allowing his love to consume you?

PRAY

*COME WITH THE FIRE OF YOUR LOVE,
LORD JESUS. BURN DOWN MY IDOLS,
MY PRIDE, MY LAZINESS, MY FEARS,
MY MISCONCEPTIONS ABOUT YOU,
MY WILLINGNESS TO SETTLE, MY
FALSEHOODS, MY SHAME, MY LIES,
THE PLACES I HAVEN'T LET LOVE IN.
SET ME ABLAZE WITH YOUR LOVE TO
SPREAD TO ALL THOSE I MEET. JESUS,
I WANT TO SHARE IN YOUR DIVINE
LIFE. AMEN.*

SECOND WEEK OF ADVENT

SATURDAY

HIS GAZE, THE TOUCH OF HIS
HEART HEALS US THROUGH
AN UNDENIABLY PAINFUL
TRANSFORMATION "AS THROUGH
FIRE." BUT IT IS A BLESSED PAIN,
IN WHICH THE HOLY POWER OF
HIS LOVE SEARS THROUGH US
LIKE A FLAME, ENABLING US TO
BECOME TOTALLY OURSELVES
AND THUS TOTALLY OF GOD.

POPE BENEDICT XVI, *SPE SALVI,* **47**

HE COMES TO BE ONE WITH US

Our local priest went to his home country of India to spend six months ministering to the local people. When he returned, he shared that one day he was preaching about God's commandment that says there shall be no other gods before him. India is said to have more than three hundred million gods, so when the people heard this message, they didn't have to wonder what idols might be in their lives; they had physical objects with names. They immediately went home, grabbed handfuls of idols in the form of statues, and brought them back to the priest. I asked the priest what he did with the idols. He flatly replied, "I put them in a big pile, then I burned them. That's what you do with idols."

An idol doesn't have to be a physical object—it's anything we turn to for satisfaction, meaning, and relief other than God. God has a jealous love for us—not jealous in a human, sinful way, but jealous in that he doesn't want separation and only half a heart. He wants a relationship that is all-in, faithful, and committed. Just as in a marriage when a couple makes a covenant and forsakes all others, God offers us everything and desires the same in return. He has moved first, given his heart, his promise, his covenant, and his life, and he waits for our response. An offering of love so powerful and good deserves a significant response from us.

To respond, we need to reflect and be honest about what else holds our affection. What idols and substitutes are we holding on to? God is always trying to give good things to us, but our hands are often too full to receive. What is in our hands other than Jesus?

His commandment is not meant to restrict us; rather, it is meant to set us free from the empty promises and bondage of idols so that we can encounter the fullness of life, love, and everything we are desperately searching for. Jesus is the only one who can offer you and me all that we are dreaming of. He is the dream, he is the life, he is the love, he is the joy—he is everything our hearts were made for. Will we let the fire of God's love consume the idols and make our hearts one with his?

Where I am holding on to idols, *Jesus, be born in me.*

REFLECT

1. What do you look to, other than God, for comfort?
2. What desire do you doubt that God can satisfy?
3. What is your response to God's gift of himself to you?

PRAY

JESUS, THERE ARE SO MANY PLACES IN MY LIFE WHERE I DON'T BELIEVE THAT YOU WILL BE ENOUGH FOR ME, SO I TURN TO OTHER THINGS IN HOPES THAT THEY WILL SATISFY. I REPENT OF ALL THE WAYS I HAVE GIVEN MY HEART TO OTHER THINGS. PLEASE BURN AWAY ALL OF MY IDOLS AND BE MY ONE AND ONLY GOD. JESUS, I WANT TO SHARE IN YOUR DIVINE LIFE. AMEN.

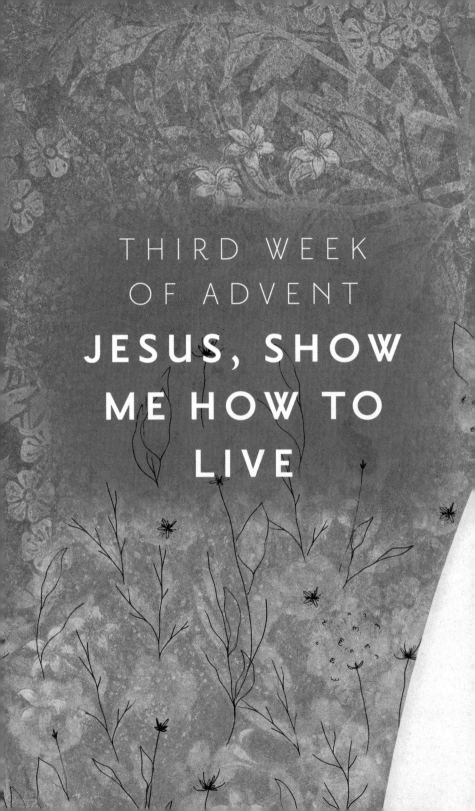

THIRD WEEK
OF ADVENT

JESUS, SHOW ME HOW TO LIVE

THIRD WEEK OF ADVENT

SUNDAY

WE HAVE THIS AS A SURE AND
STEADFAST ANCHOR OF THE
SOUL, A HOPE.

HEBREWS 6:19

HE COMES TO BE OUR HOPE

A few years ago, I watched an amazing World War II movie called *Unbroken*. It's based on the true story of a young American athlete who joins the army; while on a rescue mission, his plane crashes into the ocean. He survives on a raft for more than forty days until he is picked up by the Japanese army and imprisoned in a work camp. It's there that he is severely tortured by his captors. Although he suffered for many years in prison, his spirit remained unbroken. It's unfathomable what a person can endure if their heart is set on something bigger than their suffering, if they have a reason to hope. Through this witness it becomes clear, "The one who has hope lives differently" (Pope Benedict XVI, *Spe Salvi*, 2).

If there is one thing we have all experienced, it's that life is hard. There is a range of difficulty from the small annoying things to heart-wrenching tragedies that strike unexpectedly. Many of life's sorrows knock the breath right out of us. It doesn't seem to matter whether you're rich or poor or a friend or foe of Jesus—no one is exempt from pain. In fact, Jesus assures us in the Gospel of John that we will have trouble in this world, but the key is in what he says next, "But be of good cheer, I have overcome the world!" (Jn 16:33). There is one reason for our hope that can carry us through the deepest sufferings, and that is Jesus Christ.

The life and Cross of Jesus show us that the worst tragedies can be transformed and lead to new life. Jesus endured betrayal, friends dying, and being mocked, gossiped about, and relentlessly tortured even unto death; yet, that was not the final word. He rose from the dead! There are many who have died a heroic death, even died so another might live, but none of them rose from the dead, proving that Jesus has unmatched power even over death. Truly, he is God.

We need to be anchored to Jesus so that when things fall apart, we are secure and still have a reason to hope. Jesus wants to come into in every place of our suffering so that his power and new life can be born. We can be people of hope and have joy in the midst of our pain, knowing that suffering is not the end of the story—heaven is.

Where I have lost hope, *Jesus, be born in me.*

REFLECT

1. What places in your life do you experience hopelessness?
2. Do you trust that God can bring good out of your suffering?

_____

_____

_____

_____

_____

_____

_____

_____

_____

_____

_____

PRAY

*DEAR JESUS, I NEED YOU. HELP ME
TO ANCHOR MYSELF TO YOU, SO THAT
IN THE MIDST OF THE STORMS AND
TRIALS OF LIFE, I MAY TRUST IN YOUR
PROMISES. JESUS, BE MY HOPE AND
SHOW ME HOW TO LIVE. AMEN.*

THIRD WEEK OF ADVENT

MONDAY

PEACE I LEAVE WITH YOU; MY
PEACE I GIVE TO YOU; NOT AS
THE WORLD GIVES DO I GIVE TO
YOU. LET NOT YOUR HEARTS BE
TROUBLED, NEITHER LET THEM
BE AFRAID.

JOHN 14:27

HE COMES WITH PEACE

My pulse was racing, my body was shaking, and my mind was unraveling. I was having a panic attack. I had never experienced anything like it and was convinced that I must be having a medical emergency. My husband, who is a therapist, realized what was happening, wrapped his arms around me, and held me until it passed.

Over the next couple of years, I continued to fall apart. Panic attacks became more frequent, depression set in, and anxiety was creeping into every part of my mind and body. I went to doctors, chiropractors, naturopaths, counseling, and prayed every day. I tried everything to try to fix it, but nothing worked. When all of my tests came back negative and a neurologist told me that I didn't have anything physically wrong with me, I was left with a question, "What was causing this?" At the end of my search, I realized that at a young age, self-reliance had taken root in my life. Without realizing it, I had not been depending on God and was carrying the weight of the world on my shoulders. When I allowed God to heal my self-reliance, my anxiety and depression healed with it.

Self-reliance is a destroyer of peace. It causes us to take on the immense weight of responsibility and outcomes, without depending on God's strength and providence. We must constantly calculate and be vigilant to try to prepare for every scenario without realizing that we are behaving like an orphan, as one who doesn't have a loving Father who cares for us. We all struggle with this to some degree, and if we don't depend on God, how is he supposed to show us his immeasurable provision? In his book *Searching for and Maintaining Peace,* Fr. Jacques Philippe says, "Many do not believe in Providence because they've never experienced it, but they've never experienced it because they've never jumped into the void and taken the leap of faith."

Letting go of control and placing our trust in God leads to a life of peace. It allows God to do the heavy lifting and frees us to be children who depend on the loving care of a good Father. Jesus, the Prince of Peace, comes to shatter the heavy yoke. He comes to breathe peace into every area of our lives that we are gripping tightly. Will you allow him to love you there?

Where I lack peace, *Jesus, be born in me.*

REFLECT

1. In what area of your life do you desire peace the most?
2. What is one reason that you often rely on yourself instead of God?
3. What is one of the barriers you have to trust?
4. Take several deep breaths in and out, and as you do, invite Jesus to breathe his peace within you.

_____

_____

_____

_____

_____

_____

_____

_____

_____

_____

PRAY

_DEAR JESUS, I'M TIRED OF DEPENDING
ON MY POWER INSTEAD OF ON YOU.
LORD, I LAY DOWN MY BURDENS AT
YOUR FEET AND ASK THAT YOU WOULD
PROVIDE FOR ALL OF MY NEEDS. I
CHOOSE TO TRUST YOU AND YOUR
PLAN. JESUS, SHOW ME HOW TO LIVE.
AMEN._

THIRD WEEK OF ADVENT

TUESDAY

YOU HAVE RAVISHED MY HEART
WITH A GLANCE OF YOUR EYES.

SONG OF SOLOMON 4:9

HE COMES AS A LOVER

Recently I was looking through a love letter, and here are some of the things that I read: I love you. You are mine. I have loved you with an everlasting love. I would give up nations for you. I will make a covenant with you. Your love is better than wine. I am faint with love. You have ravished my heart. Kiss me with the kisses of your mouth. I found the one. Love is stronger than death. I have chosen you. I will be with you. Even when you turn gray, I will carry you. You will be called my delight. Let me sing for my beloved.

Maybe it's obvious, but the love letter I found these excerpts from is the Bible, God's love letter to us. These are all things that he is saying to you right now. What God is this who comes to us as a lover? Most gods are seen as tyrants, distant, or vengeful, whereas our God comes as a bridegroom with an invitation to an intimate relationship of love. This isn't a sentimental idea meant for the religious romantics, but the reality that each person is invited to respond to.

We have so many false images of God. Some are born from our imagination, and most we have interpreted through the poor examples of those who are supposed to reveal his face, but instead have tragically marred it. Whether it is a cruel judge who seeks to punish, one who is distant and uncaring, or a personal assistant to give us things, Jesus is far from any of those images. Throughout scripture, he reveals many attributes of who he is, such as king, friend, and Savior, but my favorite of all is the bridegroom, a lover.

This reality can be difficult for us because we believe God is distant or because our experience with intimacy has been so pornographized and twisted that we can't imagine intimacy with Jesus. Each of us has a Marian dimension to our souls because God desires that we would be one with him. We are made to receive Christ, and just as he entered into the womb of Mary, so too he desires to enter into our bodies and bring life. The intimacy that Jesus wants with us is pure, free, total, faithful, and life-giving. He will never force or coerce; he extends the invitation.

Where I need the love of the divine bridegroom, *Jesus, be born in me.*

REFLECT

1. What stirs in your heart as you reflect on Jesus coming to you as a lover, and how is that different from how you already view him?
2. What parts of your heart are closed to him as a lover? Why?
3. What would it look like to let Christ love you this way?

PRAY

*JESUS, LOVER OF MY SOUL, YOU
DESIRE AN INTIMATE RELATIONSHIP
WITH ME. HEAL THE PLACES WITHIN
THAT HAVE BEEN HURT BY THOSE WHO
WERE MEANT TO LOVE ME. HELP ME TO
OPEN MY HEART TO ALL OF WHO YOU
ARE. JESUS, SHOW ME HOW TO LIVE.
AMEN.*

THIRD WEEK OF ADVENT

WEDNESDAY

TELL ACHING MANKIND TO
SNUGGLE CLOSE TO MY
MERCIFUL HEART, AND I WILL
FILL IT WITH PEACE.

ST. FAUSTINA, *DIARY*, 1074

HE COMES WITH AN OPEN HEART

When we look at the life of Jesus, we see he has very real human experiences of both love and suffering. He loves everyone deeply: his friends, his mother, the broken, and even those who hate him. We know he experienced intense physical suffering and betrayal at the hands of people. Here's the thing that I can't fathom: through it all, he stays open. He stays vulnerable and open while being hurt, often knowing that more hurt is coming.

If you are anything like me, I tend to pull away and close my heart to those who hurt me. I self-protect out of fear, so they can't hurt me again. This is a very common human reaction to pain; it makes sense. This response is necessary in situations of abuse and serious harm, but I'm not referring to those types of relationships. We regularly stonewall people who are close to us in daily life, our family, coworkers, friends, and those in our community who hurt us. We close off their access to our hearts, creating a barrier to giving and receiving love, the very thing we are made for. In relationships, we as Christians aren't called to follow what "makes sense," but rather the way of Jesus.

Jesus's ways don't always make sense, his ways are not our ways, but they are the path to life. Christ doesn't want us to wall ourselves off from relationships, because it damages others and ourselves. He wants to come and transform our self-protection into self-gift and empower us to respond to those who hurt us with true charity. Vulnerability is essential to love, and vulnerability means that we stay open despite the risk of disappointment and hurt. C. S. Lewis rightly points out, "To love at all is to be vulnerable. Love anything, and your heart will certainly be wrung and possibly be broken" (C. S. Lewis, *The Four Loves*).

We are incapable of love like this on our own; we need the ocean of his love to overwhelm our fears. The way to begin is to let Christ love us like this in our brokenness. In the places we sin and hurt our relationship with him, we can experience the merciful love of Jesus who won't close his heart to us. He will stay open no matter how many times we betray him. That is precisely where he wants to love us.

Where my heart is closed, *Jesus, be born in me.*

REFLECT

1. What is one relationship where you are struggling to keep your heart open?
2. What does it look like when you close your heart to someone?
3. What would it look like for you to stay open in difficult relationships?

_____

_____

_____

_____

_____

_____

_____

_____

_____

PRAY

*JESUS, YOU ARE PERFECTLY STRONG
AND PERFECTLY VULNERABLE. PLEASE
HELP ME TO KEEP MY HEART OPEN
IN THE RELATIONSHIP WHERE I
AM EXPERIENCING HURT AND NOT
SHUT OUT THE POSSIBILITY OF
RECONCILIATION AND CHARITY.
JESUS, SHOW ME HOW TO LIVE. AMEN.*

THIRD WEEK OF ADVENT

THURSDAY

BE STILL, AND KNOW THAT I AM
GOD.

PSALM 46:10

HE COMES IN THE SILENCE

I had my fair share of punishments growing up. The worst was the silent treatment, and some people in my family were experts at it. When they were upset with me, they would stop talking, and it could last for days or longer if it was bad. It was a kind of torture. No matter what I said to make amends, they used silence to isolate me until they decided I was off the hook. Silence can wound.

Silence can also expose uncomfortable things under the surface. I have a friend who is always busy working, and when the world shut down a few years ago, I remember she became visibly rattled. Tears rose easily during conversation, and I could see the pain bubble to the surface. Busyness and noise had been the Band-Aid, and when she was faced with silence, the pain was visible.

Thus, silence can be an uncomfortable experience, which is worth acknowledging when we have a God who, as Mother Teresa says, is "the friend of silence." If we have negative experiences with silence and we go to prayer and are met with silence from God, there is a temptation to interpret it negatively. If we interpret that silence from God means we are alone to face our problems or that we are being isolated from him, then we are likely going to struggle with or avoid getting quiet. However, if we can associate silence with trust and love, we, too, can become a friend of silence and thus experience communion with God there.

Silence can be beautiful. What about the moments when we see glory in creation that leaves us speechless, or when we sit still with a dear friend savoring the safety of their presence, or when music has been played and the crowd is hushed with tear-filled eyes at its profound beauty? Silence has the power to heal and bring peace to our weary souls.

As Jesus arrives in the silence of that first holy night, I can imagine that Mary and Joseph could barely breathe when they saw him—the wonder of that moment, the unspeakable joy, and the hushed heart that found itself on sacred ground. If we allow our hearts to trust that silence with God is safe, we might experience what Joseph and Mary experienced: the profound peace and closeness that comes when we are with God in the quiet.

Where I fear silence, *Jesus, be born in me.*

REFLECT

1. What is one positive and one negative experience you have had with silence?
2. Do you often make space for silence in your day, or do you avoid it?
3. Take a moment to remove all the noise around you, and invite Jesus to come and heal any negative interpretations you may have about silence in prayer.

PRAY

DEAR JESUS, PLEASE HEAL THE PLACES IN ME THAT HAVE BEEN WOUNDED BY SILENCE. HELP ME TO TRUST THAT SILENCE IS A GIFT THAT INVITES ME INTO A DEEPER RELATIONSHIP WITH YOU. JESUS, SHOW ME HOW TO LIVE. AMEN.

THIRD WEEK OF ADVENT

FRIDAY

TRULY I TELL YOU, UNLESS
YOU CHANGE AND BECOME
LIKE CHILDREN, YOU WILL
NEVER ENTER THE KINGDOM OF
HEAVEN.

MATTHEW 18:3

HE COMES AS A CHILD

On the wall of the house I grew up in hung an image depicting Jesus with his head tilted back and laughter erupting from his mouth. His eyes were shut tight, displaying his laugh lines, and a look of pure delight was on his face. Seeing this image every day of my childhood helped shape an understanding of an often-overlooked part of God's personality: his childlike playfulness.

While the scriptures offer limited insights into the early life of Jesus, there is still much we can learn. Contemplating his childhood becomes crucial in our understanding of the heart of God, and reflecting on his human experiences can unveil profound revelations. Have you ever pondered that Jesus spent half of his life on earth as a child? What might this tell us about him, especially when he teaches us that we must become like little children to enter the kingdom of heaven? We can infer that we were never meant to lose the characteristics and heart of our childhood selves, especially the desire to play. Jesus, as a perfectly integrated person, didn't leave playfulness behind.

G. K. Chesterton says, "The true object of all human life is play. Earth is a task garden; heaven is a playground" (*All Things Considered*). Jesus was once a toddler who likely giggled uncontrollably when Joseph made funny faces at him. He would have run and played his favorite game with other children in Nazareth, and knowing the compelling nature of Jesus, he likely had an amazing sense of humor. I can only imagine how hard he made the disciples belly-laugh. Jesus, who is God, remains perfectly integrated and retains an enduring desire to play, seeking to infuse joy and laughter into our relationship with him.

Many of us can be tempted to reduce Jesus's personality to stoic and impersonal, but this would fall short in acknowledging Jesus's full humanity. Jesus, the Son of God, perfect in both divinity and humanity, expresses all of his emotions and attributes with perfect harmony, never having to subdue his personality because of fear. As we encounter the real personality of Jesus, it can reveal to us how he desires to relate to us, as well as how we are meant to relate to him and relate to ourselves. Today, may we take time to allow our hearts to see him rightly and encounter the joy and playfulness of the childlike heart of God.

Where I lack a childlike heart, *Jesus, be born in me.*

REFLECT

1. In Matthew 19:14, Jesus says, "Let the children come to me." What thoughts come to mind as you hear him say that to you?
2. Reflect on your favorite part of being a child. How could that connect to how God desires to relate to you and you to him?
3. Ask Jesus this question: "What game do you want to play with me?" Write down what he tells you, and then ask, "Why do you want to play that game with me?"

_____

_____

_____

_____

_____

_____

_____

_____

_____

_____

PRAY

*DEAR JESUS, YOU ARE INVITING ME
TO BE LIKE A CHILD AND EXPERIENCE
PLAYFULNESS IN MY RELATIONSHIP
WITH YOU. PLEASE RESTORE MY
CHILDLIKE HEART AND TEACH ME TO
HAVE JOY. JESUS, SHOW ME HOW TO
LIVE. AMEN.*

THIRD WEEK OF ADVENT

SATURDAY

I LED THEM WITH CORDS OF
HUMAN KINDNESS, WITH BANDS
OF LOVE. I WAS TO THEM LIKE
THOSE WHO LIFT INFANTS TO
THEIR CHEEKS. I BENT DOWN TO
THEM AND FED THEM.

HOSEA 11:4

HE COMES TO BE HELD

Following the C-section births of my son and daughter, my husband told me that he got to spend the most sacred time with them, because while I was recovering postsurgery, he was alone with them. He described the quiet moments when their eyes took each other in and how he would hold their face close to his while he whispered little secrets of how much he loved them—a memory that will be burned in his heart forever.

As we reflect on the birth of Jesus, we need to resist the temptation to sterilize the Incarnation. It's not only a divine encounter, but also a human experience. Jesus is fully God and fully man. Mary gives birth to Christ, and all the messy, beautiful moments happen there too. The Creator of heaven and earth is suddenly being held in the arms of Mary and Joseph. He who formed the mountains allows himself to be *held* by parents, to be rocked and soothed. Many of us can get a false impression that because God is majestic and pure, he couldn't possibly want to come too close to us. Yet here, in Jesus's birth story, we find that he comes not only as the divine Lord but also as one of us, and he wants to be drawn close amid imperfection. There is no place too lowly for him.

Let's reflect. Imagine being inside the stable in Bethlehem. It's evening and a lantern is illuminating the space. You're sitting on a stool near the wall. It's quiet, and calm has settled over everyone. Mary is curled up, resting on a bed of straw on the floor. Joseph is standing near her, holding the newborn Jesus. He walks over to you and asks, "Do you want to hold him?" His arms reach toward you, and he offers you baby Jesus. You're frozen for a moment and hear Joseph's gentle voice again as he says your name and asks with a smile, "Do you want to hold him?" You receive Jesus and place your left hand under his tiny head, while your right arm embraces his fragile body. You look down, and your eyes meet. He's staring, fixated on you. You raise him closer, place his tiny cheek on your own, and feel the warmth of his breath. The Savior, who holds the whole world in his hands, is freely allowing himself to be held by you.

Where I fear being vulnerable, *Jesus, be born in me.*

REFLECT

1. Write down what stood out to you, or ask yourself, "What did Jesus say to me during the meditation?"
2. What stirs in your heart as you think about holding Jesus?
3. Jesus wants to be close. What is one way you can invite him to come close this Advent?

PRAY

DEAR JESUS, YOU REVEAL TO US THAT YOU ARE NOT A DISTANT GOD, BUT A GOD WHO DRAWS CLOSE. HELP ME ALSO NOT TO BE DISTANT, BUT TO ALLOW MYSELF TO HOLD YOU AND BE HELD BY YOU. JESUS, SHOW ME HOW TO LIVE. AMEN.

FOURTH WEEK
OF ADVENT

JESUS, SHOW US GOD'S LOVE

FOURTH WEEK OF ADVENT

SUNDAY

JESUS HAS CHOSEN TO SHOW ME
THE ONLY WAY WHICH LEADS TO
THE DIVINE FURNACE OF LOVE;
IT IS THE WAY OF CHILDLIKE
SELF-SURRENDER, THE WAY OF
A CHILD WHO SLEEPS, AFRAID
OF NOTHING, IN ITS FATHER'S
ARMS.

ST. THÉRÈSE OF LISIEUX

HE COMES WITHOUT INTIMIDATION

I sometimes wonder why God would come as a baby. Why would he get so low to the ground, so humble, so weak, so helpless and vulnerable, when he could have come in immense power? All of those things are uncomfortable for the normal human being, and we often avoid weakness as much as possible, so why would Almighty God willingly choose to come to us like this? He could have chosen to come to earth with angel armies, with a sword in his hand, flattening the mountains and showing the breadth of his power, but he didn't.

God is not like us, and he chooses to reveal himself in approachable littleness. He takes the lowest place, dependent on human parents to feed and teach him. He comes with trust in us and literally puts his life into our hands. He doesn't come to dominate, to force his way, to coerce or trick us. He comes in the most open and simple way. He comes to love us and allows us to choose whether or not to love him back.

This is his heart, the heart of one who loves us so deeply and desires a vulnerable, trusting relationship with us. He doesn't want us to fear him, so he comes with no human strength. He doesn't want us to cower from his presence, so he makes himself smaller than us. He doesn't want us to feel unworthy, so he comes without a crown or wealth. He doesn't want us to feel as if we don't have enough, so he comes with nothing, not even clothes. He comes as a child in need of love, care, and affection.

In this example, Jesus is also modeling how we are to live in a relationship with him. We are invited to come in our poverty, weakness, and littleness—without money, status, qualifications, or a need to pretend we are better than we are. The last thing he wants to do is intimidate us. He wants to be received by us and wants us to be received by him, just as we are. He wants us to know that we are worthy of his love.

Where I feel unworthy, *Jesus, be born in me.*

REFLECT

1. What qualities of Jesus's humility speak to you (poverty, littleness, nakedness, etc.)?
2. What holds you back from coming just as you are before God?
3. Have you ever gotten the impression that God wants to intimidate you? Why or why not?

PRAY

*JESUS, YOU DON'T COME TO
INTIMIDATE US; YOU COME TO LOVE
US AND RECEIVE US JUST AS WE ARE.
MAY YOUR HUMBLE PRESENCE TEACH
ME TO BE LITTLE AND DEPENDENT ON
YOU. JESUS, SHOW ME YOUR LOVE.
AMEN.*

MONDAY

THE HUMAN HEART IS CERTAINLY
AN ABYSS OF MISERY AND SIN,
BUT GOD LIES IN ITS DEPTHS.

FR. JACQUES PHILIPPE,
SEARCHING FOR AND MAINTAINING PEACE

HE COMES TO HEAL

Recently I sat with a friend and shared with him that I was back in therapy to pursue deeper healing. I told him, "The gravity of how deep the pain and wounds go is overwhelming. It's like I'm staring into the abyss, but I know I'm not alone. Christ has been so present to me." He looked at me with wide eyes and said, "Have you heard about 'Christ of the Abyss'?" He began to tell me about an Italian artist who made an eight-foot-tall bronze statue of Jesus that he sunk to the bottom of the Mediterranean Sea. There, fifty-six feet down, is the bronze Christ with his head and arms raised toward the surface, symbolically ready to embrace anyone who finds themselves untethered in the deep dark. Tears fell down my cheek as my friend referenced Psalm 139, "Even if I go to the depths, you are there." Then he said, "No matter how deep you go, Christ is lower still." Those words came as a hopeful balm to my heart and captured what I was already experiencing: Christ is present in the depth of suffering.

We can struggle to believe the healing presence of God wants to go that deep, that he really wants to go all the way down. If we are honest, that can be scary, because allowing Christ to go all the way down means that we have to open up the places that we have shoved to the bottom, covered up with our facades, anger, control, grief, and self-righteous attitudes, and look at what's really under the surface.

If we are to be courageous with our wounds, we need the gift of faith, faith that our God has the power and the desire to heal us. In my work with people and in my own life, I have seen Jesus heal damaged hearts, deep shame, anxiety, depression, broken marriages, terminal cancer, infertility, rigid mindsets, attachment wounds, and the list goes on. One thing is for sure, the miracles of Jesus didn't just happen two thousand years ago; they are happening now. The same Jesus who healed the leper is the same Jesus who comes to you and me now. There is nowhere that he won't go. There is nothing too lost, too big, too dead, or too dark for him. Whatever lies at the bottom, Christ is deeper still, waiting for us with open arms.

Where I need your healing, *Jesus, be born in me.*

REFLECT

1. What is one area of pain that you have buried and are struggling to have hope in experiencing healing?
2. Think about one of your deepest sins, struggles, or wounds. Imagine Jesus is there with you, with his arms stretched out, holding the pain of all of it with you. What do you want to tell him? What do you think he wants to say to you?

PRAY

*JESUS, YOU DESIRE TO BRING YOUR
PRESENCE TO THE DEEPEST PLACES IN
ME WHERE PAIN AND SHAME RESIDE.
I DESPERATELY NEED YOUR HEALING
IN MY LIFE. HELP ME TO TRUST THAT
YOUR HANDS ARE THERE TO HEAL ME
AND NOT TO HURT ME. JESUS, SHOW
ME YOUR LOVE. AMEN.*

FOURTH WEEK OF ADVENT

TUESDAY

I HAVE CALLED YOU BY NAME,
YOU ARE MINE.

ISAIAH 43:1

HE COMES WITH A NAME

Our friends had a gender-reveal party where one person who knew the baby's gender ordered balloons that contained the corresponding pink or blue confetti, so when the couple gathered with their friends and popped the balloon, they experienced the revelation together. The joy that erupted when they saw the blue confetti moved me to tears. What was hidden was now known: their baby was a boy. Later, even more was revealed when they chose his name.

Jesus's birth announcement started about seven hundred years before his birth when Isaiah prophesied, "A virgin will conceive and bear a son" (Is 7:14). He goes on to reveal titles of this son: Immanuel, Wonderful Counselor, Mighty God, and Prince of Peace. Each of these titles describes the character of the Messiah who was to come. Later, when the angel appears to Mary, he announces the name the child was to be called: "You will conceive in your womb and bear a son, and you shall call his name Jesus" (Lk 1:31).

God comes with the desire to be known and to have a personal and intimate relationship with us. The *Catechism* says, "Everyone's name is sacred. The name is the icon of the person. It demands respect as a sign of the dignity of the one who bears it" (*CCC* 2158). The name *Jesus*, which means "God saves" in Hebrew, reveals to us who he is (his identity) and what he came here to do (see *CCC* 430). *Jesus*, the name that will come forth from the mouths of family, friends, followers, and even his betrayers. *Jesus*, the name that you and I can call upon at any moment. His name is like no other because "his name is the only one that contains the presence it signifies" (*CCC* 2666). When we speak the name of Jesus, he is immediately with us.

We also have been given a name and have been called many names throughout our lives. Some have blessed us, and some have wounded us, damaging our sense of our God-given glory. God wants to reveal our true identity by declaring names over us that reveal our profound worth. Throughout scripture he calls us chosen, beloved, mine, friend, child, citizen of heaven, and lover. The Lord knows you. He has called you by name, and you belong to him.

Where I need to hear you call me by name, *Jesus, be born in me.*

REFLECT

1. How do you feel when you hear the truth that God wants you to know who he is?
2. In the list of names that God has called you in scripture, which one stands out to you?
3. What damaging name have you been called that you need to reject? What name from God do you want to receive?

_____

_____

_____

_____

_____

_____

_____

_____

PRAY

*JESUS, THANK YOU FOR REVEALING
YOUR NAME TO ME AND SHOWING ME
THAT YOU ARE NOT HIDDEN AND WANT
TO BE KNOWN. HELP ME TO REMEMBER
THAT THERE IS POWER IN YOUR
NAME THAT I CAN CALL UPON AT ANY
MOMENT. ALLOW ME THE GRACE TO
BELIEVE THAT YOU HAVE CALLED ME BY
NAME AND I BELONG TO YOU. JESUS,
SHOW ME YOUR LOVE. AMEN.*

FOURTH WEEK OF ADVENT

WEDNESDAY

JESUS WEPT.

JOHN 11:35

HE COMES WITH A CRY

When each of my babies was born, the first thing I heard was their cry. As the amniotic fluid was cleared from their little lungs and they took in their first breath, a cry soon rang out in the delivery room. That was the best sound because you knew they were alive and breathing. Not all babies cry in the first seconds of being born, but soon after, they all cry. The Christ child would have been no different.

The prophets in the Old Testament were anointed by God and given messages to proclaim to God's people. Essentially, they were God's voice in the world. There were many prophets throughout the scriptures, but have you ever wondered how much time passed between the last prophesy about the coming Messiah in the Old Testament and the birth of Jesus in the New Testament? Malachi was the last known Old Testament prophet, and we know that he lived around 450 BC. This means that there were likely about four hundred years of silence, where no one heard God's voice through prophets. Then one night, in the darkness, a cry rang out and broke the silence. One of the first things that humanity hears from God in four hundred years is his real human voice, and he cries. The Christ child sums up God's four hundred years of silence in a cry.

We know enough about God's desire for union with humanity that we can imagine that God's crying is meant to speak a truth to us. As we have reflected before, God is in the details. He could have chosen to come with a full vocabulary if he wanted to and to tell us everything that was on his mind. So I would think that his first sounds from his mouth would be important. Why is one of the only ways that God could express himself in his frail infant state with a cry? What if he had a lot of reasons to cry? What if his longing for us to be with him forever almost hurts? What if the one who was there in the beginning and watched the fall of humanity found it painful to watch us suffer? What if God's heart ached for us to be one? What if he was crying out for you?

Where I ache for union with you, *Jesus, be born in me.*

REFLECT

1. What does the image of God crying stir in your heart?
2. How do you feel when you hear the truth that God longs for you?

PRAY

*JESUS, YOUR HUMAN EMOTIONS
REVEAL TO US THAT YOU ARE A GOD
WHO FEELS WITH US AND WHO IS
MOVED BY COMPASSION FOR US. MAY
THE COMFORT OF YOUR PRESENCE
HEAL THE PLACES WHERE I AM STILL
SEPARATED FROM YOU. GIVE ME THE
GIFT OF TRUE SORROW FOR THE WAYS I
AM STILL FAR FROM YOU. JESUS, SHOW
ME YOUR LOVE. AMEN.*

FOURTH WEEK OF ADVENT

THURSDAY

"AND HIS NAME SHALL BE
CALLED EMMANUEL" (WHICH
MEANS, GOD WITH US).

MATTHEW 1:23

HE COMES TO BE WITH US

Imagine the scene. Jesus knocks on the door of the home of his friends Martha and Mary. Martha opens the door, and before he can say hello, she briskly turns and runs back to her boiling pot of food so it doesn't bubble over and yells over her shoulder, "Come in! We are glad you're here!" Jesus laughs, and as he steps through the doorway he is suddenly met with Mary's arms wrapping around him. "Good to be with you, Mary," he says, as he kisses the top of her head. As Martha busily sets the table, Mary seats Jesus at their best chair. Although another chair sits opposite him, she hesitates to be even a few feet away. He notices her reluctance and whispers, "Stay," as he gives her a wink. A bashful grin crosses her face, and she falls into a heap on the floor, letting out a giggle as she topples over onto his feet. Martha, out of breath, arrives with a cup of water for Jesus. She glances down at Mary and rolls her eyes in disappointment as if to say, "Oh sure, you sit there, while I take care of everything else." Mary, oblivious, leans her forehead on Jesus's knee. She closes her eyes as he lovingly strokes her hair. Mary sighs and thinks to herself, "I never want him to leave."

In scripture, we can see that both women are trying to love Jesus. Martha is doing so much for Jesus, but scripture says that she is distracted and worried. Whatever good intentions Martha has, her actions are causing her to miss the real thing her heart is longing for. Instead of allowing herself just be with Jesus, she stays busy and turns to resentment.

We can interpret Jesus's response as dismissive of Martha's efforts, but he is actually trying to love her into freedom. He's exposing where she is in bondage to busyness and worry. The remedy for this is not doing more—it's being with. Christ is called Emmanuel, God with us, and this "being with" is precisely the key to peace, freedom, and intimacy that Martha and all of us are longing for. As Jesus reflects on the experience of Martha and Mary, he simply says, "There is need of only one thing" (Lk 10:42). The one thing we need is simply being and allowing his presence to be with us.

Where I'm afraid to be still, *Jesus, be born in me.*

REFLECT

1. What areas of your life do you tend toward "doing" instead of "being"?
2. Imagine yourself being Mary in the scene described above. What do you want to say to Jesus? What do you want to hear him say to you?
3. How can you make time each day to "be" with Jesus?

PRAY

LOVING SAVIOR, I'M SO GRATEFUL THAT YOU DESIRE TO BE WITH ME. PLEASE HELP ME TO BRING MY DISTRACTIONS, ANXIETIES, AND BUSYNESS AND LAY THEM AT YOUR FEET. MAY I ALWAYS LOOK FOR PEACE IN YOUR PRESENCE INSTEAD OF IN MY ACTIONS. JESUS, SHOW ME YOUR LOVE. AMEN.

FOURTH WEEK OF ADVENT

FRIDAY

GOD IS NOT DISTANT: HE IS
"EMMANUEL," GOD-WITH-US.
HE IS NO STRANGER: HE HAS A
FACE, THE FACE OF JESUS.

**POPE BENEDICT XVI,
CHRISTMAS DAY ADDRESS 2010**

HE COMES AS A
PERSON WITH A FACE

In a recent interview, I had to respond to a lightning round of questions and say the first thing that came to mind. The first question was "If you could ask God one question, what would it be?" Without a beat, I blurted out: "Can I see your face?" My answer took me by surprise, but as I reflected on it, I realized this is a deep longing I have. This isn't unique to me; it's a universal human desire. God has placed in us a desire to see him and be seen by him.

In the Old Testament, there is a striking story about Moses being on a mountain and expressing his desire to see God. "Show me your glory," he said. God responded by telling Moses that if he were to look upon him, he would die. Therefore, Moses was to hide until God passed by, and then he could only look at the Lord's back. God is so pure and holy that, before the coming of Christ, if we in our sinful state were to look at him, we would die. In his mercy toward man, God hid himself from us—until the Incarnation. God always desired that we would know him, and in the Garden of Eden, Adam and Eve were able to see him until sin ruptured their union. In taking on human nature, Jesus, the Son of God, becomes one of us, becomes accessible to us, and for the first time since the Garden, we can look upon God's face.

At this very moment, Jesus has a body and a face. One day, if we go to heaven, we will get to see his beautiful face. We will get to look into his eyes; we will see his lips break into a smile and laughter burst from his mouth. We will get to watch every facial expression take shape, and we will get to hug him and be held by him. Our forehead will be able to rest against his forehead, and we will feel the comfort of being close to his body. We will hold his nail-marked hands and draw close to his pierced side. We will see his feet that walked the dirt roads of Galilee, that were washed by Mary Magdalene, and that were fastened to the Cross for you and me. Our glorious and holy God isn't all mystery—he has a face and wants us to see him.

Where I need to see your face, *Jesus, be born in me.*

REFLECT

1. Take a moment to reflect. What do you imagine Jesus's face looks like?
2. Imagine yourself going to heaven and seeing Jesus for the first time. What is the first thing you want to do? What does he do when he sees you?

_____

_____

_____

_____

_____

_____

_____

_____

_____

_____

PRAY

_JESUS, I DESIRE TO SEE YOU AND BE
SEEN BY YOU. I DESIRE TO KNOW YOU
AND BE KNOWN BY YOU. OPEN MY EYES
TO TRULY SEE YOU FOR WHO YOU ARE
AND TO RECEIVE YOUR LOVING GAZE
UPON ME. JESUS, SHOW ME YOUR
LOVE. AMEN._

FOURTH WEEK OF ADVENT

SATURDAY

THE HOLY SPIRIT WILL COME
UPON YOU, AND THE POWER
OF THE MOST HIGH WILL
OVERSHADOW YOU.

LUKE 1:35

HE COMES WITH
THE HOLY SPIRIT

Before the creation of the world, the Holy Spirit hovered. Before the apostles received the power to forgive sins, the Holy Spirit was breathed on them. Before the gifts of Pentecost were released upon the disciples, the Holy Spirit rested upon them. Before the Baptism of Jesus, the Holy Spirit descended, and before the Incarnation of Jesus, the Holy Spirit overshadowed Mary.

As we prepare to welcome the gift of Jesus this Christmas, who comes to be born in us, we are also invited to open our hearts to the gift of the Holy Spirit. While we focus much of our attention during Advent on the person of Jesus, who scripture tells us reveals the Father, we have the Spirit who also desires to be one with us. For us to truly encounter Christ, we must be open to "the Spirit of truth who 'unveils' Christ to us" (*CCC* 687).

This same Spirit wants to dwell within us and release all of his power like a river flowing through our lives and out into the world. Although many of us have received the gift of the Spirit at Baptism and Confirmation, we must not view these as isolated moments, but rather as the beginnings of a life that is active in the Spirit. We see this docility and openness to the Spirit lived vibrantly in the lives of the saints and holy men and women throughout the ages.

As the Spirit came upon Mary at the Incarnation, he also came with all the strength of his presence to give her courage and all that she needed to give her full fiat to the work of God in her life. The same is true for us: when we give the Spirit permission, he comes with all of his gifts, charisms, power, council, comfort, and love so we might fully live out the plans that God has for us. This is the real adventure—to say yes with all of our hearts and be empowered with divine life to actually accomplish God's will on earth. On this Christmas Eve, may we welcome the gift of the Holy Spirit who says to us today, "Behold, I am doing a new thing" (Is 43:19).

Where I need the gift of your Holy Spirit, *Jesus, be born in me.*

REFLECT

1. When you imagine the Spirit coming upon you with all the strength of his presence, what virtue or comfort do you desire him to impart to you?
2. In what way will you say *yes* to Jesus this Christmas?

_____

_____

_____

_____

_____

_____

_____

_____

_____

_____

PRAY

HOLY SPIRIT, WHO OVERSHADOWED OUR LADY FOR CHRIST TO BE BORN IN HER WOMB, COME AND OVERSHADOW ME NOW. MAY CHRIST BE BORN IN ME, TOO. PLEASE COME WITH YOUR PRESENCE AND UNVEIL THE SON TO ME. JESUS, SHOW ME YOUR LOVE. AMEN.

CHRISTMAS DAY

THE BIGGEST GIFT THAT GOD
MADE TO MEN WAS TO SEND HIS
ONLY SON, JESUS CHRIST.

BL. CARLO ACUTIS

HE COMES AS A
GIFT TO THE WORLD

I've always been struck by the fact that even though Christmas is Jesus's birthday, he is the one who comes as the gift. Today he comes as a gift to be unwrapped, opened, and received. This Christmas and each day forward, my hope for all of us is that there would be a gift exchange between us and Jesus. This is the true keeping of the covenant.

In the Old Testament God says that he wants to make a covenant with us, his people. A covenant is different than a contract in that a contract is an agreement about the exchange of goods or services, but a covenant is the exchange of persons. The Son of God comes with the intention of a beautiful exchange. He desires to be received and to receive you and me.

Jesus wants hearts, not things; he wants you, not what you can do. Will you offer him this gift? Would you be willing, each day, to give him the gift of yourself and to receive him as a gift? Jesus coming to be one of us, to save us, to break the power of sin and make a way, was all about one thing, the gift of himself in love. St. Francis de Sales describes the Incarnation as God's "kiss to humanity," the ultimate revelation of his love for us.

On that starlit night in Bethlehem, Christ came to earth, and at the end of time he will come again, but let us not miss the profound reality that he comes to us now, in the sacredness of this present moment. God comes to us in Jesus as pure self-gift. What response does this gift deserve other than our entire heart, our very being, our whole life being lived in worship to him? Through our prayer and holiness of life, may we cry out, in union with the angels, elders, and heavenly hosts, day and night without ceasing, "Holy, holy, holy, is the Lord God Almighty, who was and is and is to come!" (Rv 4:8).

May the gift of Jesus be received celebrated, adored, and shared. Merry Christmas.

REFLECT

1. What is one tangible way that you can receive the gift of Jesus today?
2. What is one tangible way that you can give yourself as a gift to Jesus?
3. What is one tangible way that you can share the gift of Jesus with those around you today?

_____

_____

_____

_____

_____

_____

_____

_____

_____

_____

PRAY

_JESUS, YOU ARE THE GREATEST GIFT,
EVERYTHING MY HEART LONGS FOR
AND DESIRES. YOU DESERVE MY HEART
AND ALL OF MY DEVOTION. HELP
ME TO RECEIVE THE GIFT OF YOUR
PRESENCE IN MY LIFE, AND GIVE ME
THE GRACE TO RESPOND TO THIS GIFT.
AMEN._

Where I need to be awakened, *Jesus, be born in me.*
Where I am in darkness, *Jesus, be born in me.*
Where I doubt your promises, *Jesus, be born in me.*
Where I am self-reliant, *Jesus, be born in me.*
Where I am held captive, *Jesus, be born in me.*
Where I am unreconciled, *Jesus, be born in me.*
Where I am losing the battle, *Jesus, be born in me.*

Where I need familial love, *Jesus, be born in me.*
Where I hunger for more of you, *Jesus, be born in me.*
Where I need the hope of heaven, *Jesus, be born in me.*
Where I need to live your mission, *Jesus, be born in me.*
Where I need you as my brother, *Jesus, be born in me.*
Where I need your consuming fire, *Jesus, be born in me.*
Where I am holding on to idols, *Jesus, be born in me.*

Where I have lost hope, *Jesus, be born in me.*
Where I lack peace, *Jesus, be born in me.*
Where I need the love of the divine bridegroom, *Jesus, be born
    in me.*
Where my heart is closed, *Jesus, be born in me.*
Where I fear silence, *Jesus, be born in me.*
Where I lack a childlike heart, *Jesus, be born in me.*
Where I fear being vulnerable, *Jesus, be born in me.*

Where I feel unworthy, *Jesus, be born in me.*
Where I need your healing, *Jesus, be born in me.*
Where I need to hear you call me by name, *Jesus, be born in me.*
Where I ache for union with you, *Jesus, be born in me.*
Where I'm afraid to be still, *Jesus, be born in me.*
Where I need to see your face, *Jesus, be born in me.*
Where I need the gift of your Holy Spirit, *Jesus, be born in me.*

HEATHER KHYM is the cohost of the internationally popular *Abiding Together* podcast and the author of *Abide*. She and her husband, Jake, are the cofounders of Life Restoration Ministries, where she serves as director of vision and ministry of the British Columbia–based apostolate. She also serves as director of the Celtic Cross Foundation.

Heather has more than twenty-five years of experience as a speaker and retreat leader offering workshops and conferences in the United States and Canada. She attended Franciscan University of Steubenville, where she studied theology and catechetics.

She lives with her husband and three children in British Columbia, Canada.

liferestoration.ca
abidingtogetherpodcast.com
Twitter: @abidingpodcast
Instagram: @heatherkhym
YouTube: Abiding Together Podcast

JOSIAH HENLEY is a Catholic illustrator and designer. His work is featured in *Behold: A Guided Advent Journal for Prayer and Meditation* and *Return: A Guided Lent Journal for Prayer and Meditation*.

He earned a master's degree in architecture from Portland State University. His work is inspired by the ancient art and architecture of the Church, and he aims to create contemporary images that honor her tradition.

He lives with his family in Portland, Oregon.

heartofiesvs.etsy.com
Instagram: @heartofiesvs

Encountering Emmanuel
Companion Resources and Videos

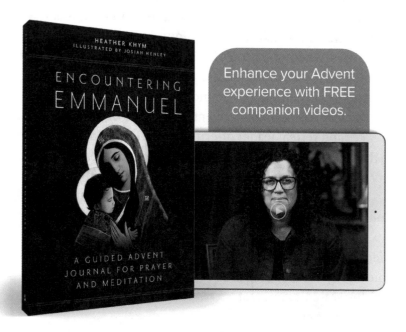

Enhance your Advent experience with FREE companion videos.

These FREE resources make this book perfect for individuals, parishes, small groups, and classrooms:

- weekly companion videos with Heather Khym
- *Encountering Emmanuel Leader's Guide*
- pulpit and bulletin announcements
- downloadable flyers, posters, and digital graphics
- and more

Scan here to access the free resources and videos or visit
avemariapress.com/private/page/encountering-emmanuel-resources